Red Madonna - 1990
Dunstan St Omer

Red Madonna - 1990
Dunstan St Omer

Roseau Valley

AND OTHER POEMS FOR BROTHER GEORGE ODLUM

AN ANTHOLOGY

Jubilee Trust Fund
Castries, St. Lucia.
2003

The Jubilee Trust Fund thanks:
The family of Harold Simmons for use of "Albertha" by Harold Simmons (1914-1966)
Dunstan St. Omer for use of "Red Madonna" – frontispiece
Llewellyn Xavier for use of "Dancing Pitons"
Virginia Henry for use of "Tambo"
Corine George for use of "Kabawé" - cover illustration
The family of the late Leo 'Spa' St. Helene (1927 - 1988) and Alwyn St. Omer for use of photograph, "Papa Jab"
The Odlum family and the Crusader newspaper for use of photographs of George Odlum.
Cecil Fevrier for digital photographs of art reproductions.
All the writers who have contributed their work (see Acknowledgements)
Kendel Hippolyte for translations of Kwéyòl poems and for general support.
Patricia Charles for proof reading.

George Odlum, who has given his full support to the publication of this anthology and the creation of the George Odlum Grant for creative artists. All proceeds from sale of this book will go to that Grant, which will be managed by the Jubilee Trust Fund.

compiler & editor John Robert Lee
book production Right Angle Imaging
book design Marlon John
printer Zenith Services Ltd

The orthography (writing system) used for the Kwéyòl poems is that developed by the Folk Research Centre and related agencies.

Cover Painting **Kabawé** (1993) - Corine George

ISBN 976-8180-74-9 (pbk)

For **BROTHER GEORGE ODLUM**
24th June 1934 - September 28th 2003
in gratitude for his lifelong contribution to the arts and culture of St. Lucia.

*'My mother is a rose,
my father is a magrit,
I myself, I am the root of flowers."*
- Sessenne Descartes

For BROTHER GEORGE ODLUM

24th June 1934 - September 28th 2003

in gratitude for his lifelong contribution
to the arts and culture of St. Lucia.

"My mother is a rose,
my father is a magril,
I myself, I am the root of flowers."

- Sesenne Descartes

ILLUSTRATIONS

Dunstan St. Omer   *"Red Madonna"*   **Frontispiece**
Harold Simmons (1914-1966)   *"Albertha"*   **p.5**
Virginia Henry   *"Tambo"*   **p.18**
Llewellyn Xavier   *"Dancing Pitons"*   **p.32**
Leo 'Spa' St. Helene
(1927-1988)   *"Papa Jab"*   **p.48**
St. Lucia Arts Guild Production
(1968)   *"Sea at Dauphin"*   **p.64**

FOREWORD   *Msgr. Dr. Patrick 'Paba' Anthony*
PROLOGUE

Dame Marie Sessenne Descartes   *Songs: (i) Nou tout sé menm*   **p.1**
   (ii) Yes, yes, it's true (É-wi sa vwé)

Charles Cadet   *Poinsettia Blossoms*   **p.3**
Ronald Boo Hinkson   *Burning eyes and hungry bellies*   **p.4**
George 'Fish' Alphonse   *Forget dem old ting*   **p.6**
Patrick 'Paba' Anthony   *Twilight*   **p.8**
Adrian Augier   *Comerette*   **p.9**
Edward Baugh (Jamaica)   *Black sand*   **p.10**
John Blanchard   *Fading lifestyle*   **p.11**
Kamau Brathwaite (Barbados)   *The visibility trigger*   **p.12**
Martin Carter (Guyana, 1927-1997)   *Proem*   **p.14**
Tassia Channel Clement   *Under the sun*   **p.15**
Melania Daniel   *Mystery lover*   **p.16**
Anderson Desir   *I have flung fire*   **p.17**
Irvin Desir   *from Islander*   **p.19**
Sheila Desmond   *Overheard*   **p.21**
Mac Donald Dixon   *Fallen angel*   **p.25**
J. Edsel Edmunds   *Them and I*   **p.24**
Hunter J. Francois   *Johnny and I*   **p.25**

Stanley French   *Fern Gully*   **p.26**
Michael Gilkes (Guyana)   *Sonnets*   **p.27**
George Goddard Jr.   *Fig vèt*   **p.29**
Melchoir Henry   *If I am angry*   **p.30**
Kendel Hippolyte   *Like wind*   **p.31**
Ras Isley   *Speak your mind*   **p.33**
barbara jacobs-small   *Breaking covenant*   **p.35**
Moses 'Musa' JnBaptiste   *Pwézèvé yo*   **p.36**
Marcian W.E. JnPierre   *Flè wòz tjè mwen*   **p.38**
Jane King   *For Fergus*   **p.39**
George Lamming (Barbados)   *Birthday poem*   **p.40**
Darnley Lebourne   *Wévolousyon an lavi*   **p.42**
John Robert Lee   *from Canticles*   **p.44**
Egbert Lucien   *Lines for a conservative*   **p.46**
Nkrumah Ayodele Lucien   *Eternal slave*   **p.47**
Armelle Mathurin   *Yè èk jòdi*   **p.49**
Yasmin Solitahe Odlum   *Last supper*   **p.51**
Lucius Prescott   *My poems*   **p.52**
Lisa Prospere   *my.times.in.your.hands.*   **p.53**
Arthur A. Raymond   *Insights*   **p.55**
Hazel Simmons-McDonald   *Parasite*   **p.56**
Kester Small   *...but until then*   **p.57**
Gandolph St. Clair   *Don Quixote*   **p.58**
Patricia Turnbull   *Rugged vessels*   **p.59**
Derek Walcott   *Roseau Valley*   **p.60**
Travis Weekes   *Tete Chemin*   **p.63**

EPILOGUE
Charles Cadet   *Ode to an artist*   **p.65**

CONTRIBUTORS   **p.67**
ACKNOWLEDGEMENTS (Authors)   **p.70**

It is a gift to recognize the extraordinary in the everyday. Persons, places, things become so familiar, we often take them for granted. Even the great can be leveled to the commonplace, leaving no room for appreciation of their unique contribution to our lives. In a small town where a Nobel Laureate can greet you in a market, and an internationally recognized musician or painter cross the street ahead of you, it is easy to lose significances, to miss the special illumination of the historical moment. **Roseau Valley and other poems for Brother George Odlum** attempts to celebrate one such moment, the life of George William Odlum. He was a major political figure in St. Lucia from the late sixties up to his death in September 2003.

This anthology — a Jubilee Trust Fund project — grew out of an insight from one its Trustees, John Robert Lee, the St. Lucian poet. Lee suggested that the Trust Fund should follow up its recent successful production of Mbongeni Ngema's SARAFINA with a book to honour George Odlum, who was then terminally ill. The Trust readily concurred, recognizing George Odlum's contribution, not only to political and social life, but also to the arts and culture of St. Lucia. He was a contemporary of Harold Simmons, Derek and Roderick Walcott, Leo 'Spa' St. Helene, Dunstan St. Omer, Garth St. Omer and that generation who led St. Lucia's Golden Age in the arts, literature and theatre.

George Odlum was alive when the compilation began. He has since passed on, giving added importance to the publication. He was an actor, director, producer of local theatre and a member of the famous St. Lucia Arts Guild. He was the owner and editor of the **Crusader** newspaper which shaped the thinking of several generations of modern St. Lucians. For many years he wrote incisive reviews of theatre and literature in local newspapers. Several St. Lucian artists — writers, actors, directors, painters, dancers, musicians, journalists — received encouragement from him as he helped to shape a group whose work spoke out of, and to, their society. And this, during the turbulent days of the seventies in the Caribbean. This anthology of poetry is offered in gratitude for his contribution to St. Lucian arts and culture. Proceeds from its sale will go towards a George Odlum Grant for creative artists, administered by the Jubilee Trust Fund.

This anthology brings together a wide selection of voices — local, regional and international. Some are seasoned poets, while others are writers for whom poetry is more a private obsession than a public profession. T.S.Eliot admonishes, "poetry must not stray too far from the ordinary everyday language which we use and hear…it cannot afford to lose its contact with the changing language of common

intercourse..." Richard Ellmann and Robert O'Clair, introducing the **Norton Anthology of Modern Poetry** have written, "The most acute rendering of an era's sensibility is its poetry." And Derek Walcott, in his book-length poem **Tiepolo's Hound** (2000) says, "Whatever the age is, it lies in the small spring of poetry everywhere."

In an age filled with distracting noise, we are exhorted to listen to the voices of our poets. This compilation contains poems in St. Lucian Kwéyòl (translated by poet Kendel Hippolyte,) standard English, and Caribbean vernacular or "nation-language." Five well-established Caribbean writers who knew Odlum, including Kamau Brathwaite and George Lamming, add a poignant dimension. The reader will find lyrics of traditional songs, popular during the George Odlum era in St. Lucia. Uniquely, this book is also a collector's item of rare paintings and photographs, by people like Harold Simmons and Leo 'Spa' St. Helene. Overall, the poems and art become a mirror that reflects the breadth of Odlum's life and that of his peers. The collection is structured like a play, with a musical prologue, and a fitting epilogue by singer and song-writer Charles Cadet, all dedicated to a "man of words" and action, who was also a talented creative artist. If one finds in this anthology, echoes of George's story, a glimpse of contemporary St. Lucian history, we will be pleased.

The Jubilee Trust Fund, publisher of this work, was established in 1997, for the promotion and support of activities and research whose aims are the enhancement of cultural and human development in St. Lucia. The Fund is intended to have a preferential option for projects supportive of the marginalized sectors of the society such as street ministry, the poor and elderly, youth at risk, and for research activities in the arts and culture. In the light of our objectives, we are particularly pleased to collaborate with the National Community Foundation (NCF) on this book project. By means of a memorandum of understanding, we are committed to working with the NCF in other areas of the arts and culture that will benefit our nation.

Sincere thanks to all the writers, artists, musicians, sponsors and other collaborators in this project. We single out Barbara Jacobs Small and Right Angle Imaging for consistent support from the inception. Profound thanks to Yasmine Solitahe and other members of the Odlum family, who, like George himself, were delighted with the idea. Thanks to the Trustees of the Jubilee Trust Fund, especially John Robert Lee, compiler and editor, whose tiny seed of an idea has blossomed into a marking out of the life of a unique man, through the words and art of his St. Lucian and Caribbean contemporaries. I like to think that we have been used to present one of George's last gifts to his beloved St. Lucia and the Caribbean.

October 2003
Castries, Saint Lucia.

SONGS

(i) Nou tout sé menm

Nou tout sé menm
Mwen di nou tout sé menm
Nou tout sé menm
Mwen di nou tout sé menm

Piti kon gwan
Jenn kon vyé
Ni wich, ni pòv
Mwen di tout sé menm

Ès ou konpwann sa?
Ès ou konpwann sa?
Ès ou konpwann sa?
Mwen di nou tout sé menm

Nou sé Sent Lisyen
Mwen di nou tout sé menm

(We are all the same
We are all the same
I say we are all the same
We are all the same
I say we are all the same

Small or great
Young or old
Whether rich or poor
We are all the same

Do you understand this?
Do you understand this?
Do you understand this?
I say we are all the same

We are all Saint Lucians
We are all the same)

Translation by Kendel Hippolyte

(ii) Yes, yes, it's true.(É-wi sa vwé)

Chantwèl:
If I tell you that affair grieved me
you can believe it's true,
If I tell you you tore up my heart,
you can say yes, it's true.
If I tell you you pierced me
you can believe I tell the truth.
Young people of today,
you do not make your love for nothing.

I met you on the highway
I met you there, you were all broken up,
I took you, I brought you to my own home
gave you food, gave you drink.
I took you to the store
bought all you needed.
Yet you still thought I wasn't doing enough,
you took your bundle and left.

Chorus:
When I tell you you brought me grief
you can believe it's true.
Did I say you tore apart my heart?
But yes, it's true!
If I tell you you penetrated me,
you got through me,
you can say yes, yes it's true.
O the children of today
they find love as nothing.

Translation by J.R. & Veronica Lee

POINSETTIA BLOSSOMS

CHARLES CADET

Ginger soaking for the ginger beer
Rich red sorrel, bottled, waiting there
Punches, puddings, cloves and spices there
Cardboard lanterns, scenes of yesteryear
Christmas carols heard everywhere
Only bring memories
This time of year.

Chorus:
Poinsettia blossoms, rich red bloom
How she loved those velvet Christmas blooms
Poinsettia blossoms, speak to my love
Tell her of my love
Bring her back to me.

Church bells ringing on a midnight clear
Organ music filling all the air
Children waiting toys from those who care
Weeping willows Christmas gifts will wear
Friendly wishes, joy, peace, good cheer
Only bring memories
This time of year.

Chorus:

BURNING EYES AND HUNGRY BELLIES

RONALD 'BOO' HINKSON

There've been times when I had to look to the sky
so the Creator could see my face
and remember me too
who He brought into this place.
With better days nowhere in sight
it seemed a never-ending fight.

Chorus:

Let's get rid of them

burning eyes and a hungry belly

and save the children of tomorrow
the tears and the sorrow

burning eyes and a hungry belly

I never ever heard of a sweet misery

burning eyes and a hungry belly

could make an angel a lion and a preacher a killer

burning eyes and a hungry belly

find its solution in a revolution
let's get rid of them
burning eyes and a hungry belly.

To need mere basics
that make life worth it
like some grub to welcome the morning sun
and then discover today
that there will be none
makes it really hard to raise a smile
if even just for a little while.

Chorus:

Albertha *(194?)*
Harold Simmons (1914 - 1966)

Albertha (1942)
Harold Simmons (1914 - 1966)

FORGET DEM OLD TING

(for Pa Bear, Pa Alphonse, Pashool)

GEORGE 'FISH' ALPHONSE

I leave all dem donkey years
through fears
through blood
through sweat and tears
through rain, through pain.
Now dem want me
jump from the frying pan
into the fire.

They say:
"get out of this village
we pass that stage
it's a new clear age.
Move into the city
you need electricity
that will help your sanity —
don't be stubborn
think urban.

This house upside down
change it round
put carpet on the ground.

Get a colour television
get cable vision
that will help your vision —
sail with the tide
blow with the wind.

Forget dem coal pot
get a gas stove
dem charcoal
make your hand black
like slavery.
You need micro-wave —
don't be foolish!

You need refrigerator
and generator;
spring mattress ends stress,
Posturepedic ends epidemic,
backache, headache, toothache.

Forget dem hand washing
it's a brand new world of machine

get a washing machine.
Dash way dem pit toilet, you need proper outlet
you need a swimming pool to keep you cool.
Be elegant, get an eleganté;
t'row way dem elephant underpants
be brief
get some string briefs!

And forget dem storytelling
stop playing dem drum
that sound like a dumb bell;
dem silly bèlè dance
dat quadrille dance —
man, do the break dance!
And, Fish, get a stereo-cd-gram!
You too damn stereotype!

Now listen,
forget dem bush tea
dem herbs tea
black local café
and de mud colour coco tea —
get some Milo
and go, go, go
for good health
and enjoy your wealth."

From time me small
me learn
that common sense born before book sense.
Never change an old for a new
cos old *kanawi* cook good food.
New broom sweeps clean
but, old broom know de corners.
Above all, me never hang me hat
where me hand cannot reach.

TWILIGHT

PATRICK 'PABA' ANTHONY

"Wandering between two worlds, one dead,
the other powerless to be born…"
Matthew Arnold. *Stanzas from the Grande Chartreuse*

I see you in the shadows of my mind
teasing the gentle waves
etching on rocks with the evening's gold

'we have found praise.'

Two gulls in graceful rhythm
herald the green flash
elusive joy, climactic.

That canoe adrift in the twilight
solitary omen
we did not see despite your odysseys
so familiar with suffering.

So much you brought me
taught me of love
and I was healed.
While you, wounded,

journeying through many dyings
calling one name, now leprous, now nameless.

Lone voyager, I travel on
jaws locked in wisdom, head
throbbing with memory
that comforts, that enslaves.

Our tale,
twilight of pain
incapable of sleep
unable to awake.

COMERETTE

ADRIAN AUGIER

Here at Comerette, named perhaps for birds
seeking the memory of the sea in watery descents,
we are nomads in a green saddle between hills,

Harboured by seas, counseled by wind,
clocked by a sun burning silently
through layers of muslin sky.

Here waves beat their diurnal rhythm
against a wilderness of salt air and sea grapes
and sand evolving into green

Savannes un-colonized despite the urban crawl
nibbling at their inland fringes, at their slow-growing seasons
in a land where all horizons flatten into blue.

In the haze, my three children climb the craggy mornes,
pressed by the wash of salty air
like cedar trees to the swept-up slopes:

A cameo of the small, diluted tribe we have become;
body language mixed by blood and history arriving from the sea
in a land where all horizons flatten into blue.

Now I pray beside the sea
that the rush of summers would slow to single frames
that the tribe may yet inherit the old memories;

That the urban creep of streetlights
will not banish all our spirits to some green blackness;
that the drumming of Atlantic breakers

On this ochre chest of coast
will always meet the cords of cedar
on the high path over mornes;

That children will also think of frigates as sizzo
and seek reclusive reef bwigo, and
find the kayal in the purple estuaries

of valleys scooping out the studded silver sea
and know the squatting sun upon their shoulders
in this land where horizons also rise from flattened blue.

BLACK SAND

EDWARD BAUGH
Jamaica

If the poem could open itself out, could be wide
as this beach of black sand, could absorb
like black sand the sun's heat, and respond
to bright sunlight with refractions of tone,
nuances that glamour would miss, if this
could happen, if the poem could yield
like black sand, if you looked patiently,
polished stones that fit in the palm
of a woman's hand, could be cool as the sand
where the waves splash gleefully over her feet,
if the poem could be open like this beach to the breeze,
like these trees that have known great winds,
if the poem could be wide and open, like a love
that is larger than desire, larger than fear,
if the poem could be patient and wide as this evening,
this beach of black sand expecting the night
without fear, the moon lifting over the sea,
the largo of sunset spreading over the city
as the jagged, wounding edges of our unworthiness
are worn down by forgiveness, wave after untiring wave…

FADING LIFESTYLE

It is
      here
every morning
where the sound of water
      flows
in a silvery line
on coffee-cups and loud-sounding *poes*
and down his naked spine.

The aroma
of strong black coffee
      at dawn
carrying in the air—
preparation for school
climbing up — down —
      then level
the maze of a usual 8 o'clock street.

At night
listening to the night symphony of tiny creatures
after pans, tea cups, plates
and feet are done

and seeks rest
we both hear from our separate rooms
the crickets, clak-claks, toads,
      all voices conducted by swaying coconut branches…

No more sweet music
no more raids on the mango palwi tree on the headmaster's estate
no more sea grapes, corn, fat-poke, cane, jack-spaniards,
no more returning!
For here he stands behind the BWIA counter
my dear mango palwi partner
      raider-bosom friend-troublemaker—
grasping his grip
straightening his tied neck
watching his watch
      a fading lifestyle!
"From here to Barbados to New York."
Never to come back home to stay.

THE VISIBILITY TRIGGER

(for Kwame Nkrumah & the leaders of the Third World)

KAMAU BRATHWAITE
(Barbados)

and so they came up over the reefs

up the creeks & rivers
oar prong put-put
hack tramp silence

and i was dreaming near morning

i offered you a kola nut
your fingers huge & smooth & red
and you took it your dress makola blue

and you broke it into gunfire

the metal was hot & jagged
it was as if the master of bronze
had poured anger into his cauldron

and let it spit spit sputter
and it was black spark green in my face
it was as if a maggot had slapped me in the belly

and i had gone soft like the kneed of my wife's bread

i could hear salt leaking out of the black hole of kaneshie
i could hear grass growing around the edges of the green lake
i could hear stalactites ringing in my cave of vision

bats batting my eyes shut
their own eyes howling like owls in the dead dark

and they marched into the village
and our five unready virginal elders met them

bowl calabash oil carafe of fire silence

and unprepared & venerable I was dreaming mighty wind in trees
our circles talismans round hut round village cooking pots

the world was round & we the spices in it
time wheeled around our memories like stars

yam cassava groundnut sweetpea bush
and then it was yams again

birth child hunter warrior
and the breath

that is no more

which is birth which is child which is hunter which is warrior
which is breath

that is no more

and they brought sticks rods roads bullets straight objects

birth was not breath
but gaping wound

hunter was not animal
but market sale

warrior was child
that is no more

and i beheld the cotton tree
guardian of graves rise upward from its monument of grass

crying aloud in its vertical hull
calling for crashes of branches vibrations of leaves

there was a lull of silver

and then the great grandfather gnashing upwards from its
teeth of roots. split down its central thunder

the stripped violated wood crying aloud its murder. the
leaves'
frontier signals alive with lamentations

and our great odoum
triggered at last by the ancestors into your visibility

crashed
into history

 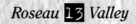

PROEM

Martin Carter
Guyana, 1927-1997

Not, in the saying of you, are you
said. Baffled and like a root
stopped by a stone you turn back questioning
the tree you feed. But what the leaves hear
is not what the roots ask. Inexhaustibly,
being at one time what was to be said
and at another time what has been said
the saying of you remains the living of you
never to be said. But, enduring,
you change with the change that changes
and yet are not of the changing of any of you.
Ever yourself, you are always about
to be yourself in something else ever with me.

UNDER THE SUN

TASSIA CHANNEL CLEMENT

Under the sun
Under the shak shak trees
Is where I dream
Dream of pretty blue bays
Orange horizons
And some green mountains

Under the sun
Is a land I call home
And in this land
Rivers sing joyous songs
And their every word
Interprets my dreams

Under the sun
On this ancient island
The birds listen
To the sounds of my dreams
And paint a picture
With their coloured wings

Under the sun
In all its radiance
I dream a place
Where courage conquers fear
Faith, hope and love live
Longer than all doubt

Under the sun
Under the shak shak trees
My dreams are done…
Rivers and birds will tell
That my dreams are true
That this place is here

MYSTERY LOVER

MELANIA DANIEL

Whose footsteps whisper
Secrets with my floor,
Who comes knocking
At my door?

Who's caressing my desires,
Who slips the lingerie off my feelings,
Who strokes my passion screaming
Louder than a village crier,
Who manifests to all the world
The love that lurks in my apathy?

Who storms the gates of my fantasies,
Who invades the territory of my dreams;
Saddled on my emotions,
Who comes riding my thoughts?

Mystery lover,
So many meadows of majorettes
Where jockeys gallop, racetracks
Of swooning débutantes—
Why have you chosen
To trot on my mind?

I HAVE FLUNG FIRE

ANDERSON DESIR

i have flung fire in the face of the Moon
bewitching it with mists of flame,
i have listened to the orchestrations of the sea,
waves playing violins to the pebbles of the shore
drawing long bogs of shivering water;
i have seen the Moon throw a shawl
over the cool thoughts of the Sand
wrapping them close with clouds;
all these things had i seen
to all these things had i listened
in all these things had i taken part.
But with you
i have been
all these things.

FROM ISLANDER

IRVIN DESIR

v.

Through the long day
you wait within :
crowded alleyways and bars

the echoing vehicular air
possessed and dispossessed
oblivious of your passing.

To reflect on this as return
to primordial time, as a bell
would toll and toll, its strain

is all that happens;
it fires the brightness
with its freedom.

garnered words
like leaves
glisten on the tree of man.

vi.
Then one afternoon, after the clink of mugs
after the doors and dresses that revolve

after the heady group of actors seesawing down
the road and masks and myriad merging of hands,

he could bill you with his hand and rock you,
melt the steel, outstare the blue horizon.

vii.
I shall see you through the cold shoreline
where the wind carries and slides over the sand

wherever we search death haunts us
everywhere the distracted petals have gone

our words fade, fade like mist over the mountain
our words add to the silence like lifting dust.

ix.
As a gray, gray villager worn by this world, her
head
is swathed with scarves, her waist bound with
bandanas, her pail
balances on her head, or carrying this as she
comes

rarely spills her sorrow, you are an ocean
murmuring

as it moves, you filled this cluttered room like
a handful of clove.

You say scores of friends have swept past like
fishscales,
modern mechanisms have slurred the pass of wood
doves.

Recall the live scene the chorus the shrill
chanson, far
from being solemn.

x.

No friend
there, no unmeaning
word or gesture and then
the leaf's lure only is intelligible.

Sundered, through speakers
speaking, flustered where I can
no longer think, of nothing of afternoon
as it would open on far cedars breathing in
the wind.

It will neither be
because of you or because
of the rain that has come, for the
handful of dust on him, that he became.

What would come comes
without our knowing, at daylight,
at dusk, revelation shaken from the
undergrowth, still petals spinning at its seam.

xi.
Memory returns, like the wind
its leaves of earlier instances
returns like the heaving rain on
arid plains and arid settlements.

Not only you alone, it is the green
day and the ripe dusk that has gone
beating through the air like birds,
the serpent grew thistles where I was growing.

Through shuttered windows
which wind has thrown open, look!
it is not the brightness that goes
it is the blue hill that grows deep.

OVERHEARD

for George Odlum

Dusk settles softly over Marigot Bay.
Elders whisper earthtalk on a moonlight night.
Be like the hills and the mountains
they say – strong, implacable, immovable,
rooted firmly in place—
stick to your convictions.

The tides of fortune ebb and flow
from the bay into the sea
from the sea into the bay
at times, lapping gently, caressing
the coastline where the hills descend
to the waves,
at times, lashing furiously, foaming
at the mouth of caves, eroding
the edges, inevitably.

Be like the waters of the sea
they say – flexible, ever moving,
reflect the wonders of the world,
mirror them on your surface,
intrigue them with your depths,
profound and elusive, come and go—

The winds of change blow unpredictable
across the bay
into sunfilled days
and the hills preen
in their green and flamboyant foliage
and the sea vies for attention
and is smooth as glass, and brilliant.

Sometimes, the wind draws a rain curtain
across the ridge, clouding
it with mystery, screening
it with poignancy, disturbing the calm surfaces.
Be mindful of the wind
they say – chance, luck or destiny,
it brings change,
element surprising all others.
On clear nights, a blanket of stars in the midnight sky
tucks you in by Marigot Bay –
be like the stars, a beacon to others
they say – shine the light,
illumine the needy,
aspire to the beauty inherent in your soul,
make its presence felt.

Be like all these, be yourself
they say – constant
for each given moment
changing with every other —
tread the tightrope lightly
but surely
maintain that delicate,
that precious balance
between constancy and change
change and constancy
as you make your way
reflecting on Marigot, St. Lucia,
Valhalla on the bay.

July 1985

FALLEN ANGEL

MAC DONALD DIXON

There was fire in his eyes
when his star shone—
people gathered
in droves, at his feet,
fame was the jilted
glory that swelled
his face.

He woke one morning,
on a burnt-out star,
his eyes dimmed with ash.
No one on the street
recalled his name,
the wind fanned flies
at his feet.

A razor initials a wrist
of virile prose; red verbs
congeal. He played with fire
and was torched by it.
O what a life it might
have been, had he just danced
with words.

 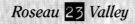

THEM AND I

J. EDSEL EDMUNDS

I live with them all,
I live with all of Them.
Them and I represent the Race,
The Human Race in Them all and I.

I, as part of Them, the Race;
Together live on in time and space,
Manifesting the norm of the Race.
But I am I in spite of Them.

The Them influence the I,
But the Them is not the I that I am;
Though the Them is the I in part,
For I am part of Them.

I must not be totally absorbed by Them,
Nor must I be Them devoid of the I as I;
For the absorption by Them
Would remove the I from I.

I am the expression of I
Not the dilution of Them.
I am the exaltation of I
In spite of the dilution by Them.

I must continue to preserve the I
In spite of the influences of Them.
I must, like Them, exert the I as I in I
Not the mirror of Them but the I in spite of Them.

JOHNNY AND I

HUNTER J. FRANCOIS

We had shared cigarettes together
Johnny and I,
And told each other jokes,
And one had come home later o'nights than the other.
And then one day he caught a fever;
Other days slipped by—
Then I saw that Johnny was slipping away
Slipping slowly and swiftly away.
So I went and called the doctor
And someone called the priest.

We had shared cigarettes together
Johnny and I,
And told each other jokes,
And one had come home later o'nights than the other—
But now I was walking through the drizzle to buy a coffin for Johnny,
And thinking of this and that,
And choosing a spot to hide the coffin away,
And urging men to dig
For the hour was near.
When I came home again they were ready to start;

I said I wouldn't go.
Then I said I would.
So I went to my room to fetch a black tie for my neck,
And a black coat for my back,
But I heard a noise of many men drawing together,
And the Foresters came and sang—
Sang in one voice a hymn for their dead brother lying there.
And a sickness came over me
For now
I knew Johnny would come home no more.
We had shared cigarettes together
Johnny and I
And told each other jokes
And one had come home later o'nights than the other.

FERN GULLY

STANLEY FRENCH

Above this tortuous trough
A river's abdicated bed
The sun sifts through a mitred
Canopy of lank arthritic trees
Clutching damp banks
In the braced wind-hushed silence
Touristic cameras click
Freezing deciduous beauty
Leaves' last shimmer
Shivering to a fall
While two ashen sweepers
Old now by the wayside move
About their work not caring
To keep pace with the perennial
Waste cascading down.

SONNETS

MICHAEL GILKES
Guyana

1.   Late Sonnet

I've written this late sonnet to say something
my shaky voice could never say to you.
But for poets past middle age, nothing
comes harder, believe me, than hunting new
metaphors. Might as well try forging
steel without the fire to make it true.
And now it's trapped on paper, this awkward thing,
even the sentiment seems paper too;
the poem a dumb creature in its cage
unable to speak as I had meant it to.
If you could free this poem from its page
you'd understand my futile ague then:
that old malarial ache, that ancient rage
that makes old men of poets, poets of old men.

2.   Carpe Diem

When I was young (as old men say) and bold,
I laughed aloud when older heads cried "carpe
diem: seize the day!" The days were mine to hold.
Now, scarred by the beak of Time, that harpy,
I find each day's a load that I must bear
alone; an ageing Atlas still down on one knee,
shoulders and arms aching with that great sphere:
the sheer, astonishing dead weight of me.
They'll say: "Married too young. Was bound to wear
his talents out with husbanding so soon."
A lie, however comforting to hear.
I gave my heart away one afternoon
when I was young and there was time to play.
Now Time has whittled all my love away.

3.   Old men should write

Old men should write, not the young in their prime:
their past's too shallow to enfranchise them.
Just so they write of lasting things, not whine
about love's fleeting, red-rose-bordered hem.
Poets have sung of love since Homer's time
and women have been pleased to find their name
immortalised in some fond poet's rhyme.
But old men should write poetry that strikes like truth,
splitting the heart in two, searing the page,
leaving an ache worse than a raging tooth.
Let them write verse that thunders, lines that rage
at having served the sentences of innocent youth
only to be set free by crooked age,
learning, too late, life's great Untruth.

5. Cathedral, Castries

He had this ringing inside his head, like bells.
Not Beethoven's divine tinnitus: more
like Michael Angel's cricket sawing away
in Vincent's ruined ear. Sunday he visited
the cathedral again. Same glow, same amber
shafts of sunlight cloudy with Cherubim.
Confessed his sin, Despair. That noise in his ear
Was Despair's maddening din. He looked at the paintings
on the walls. Sacred graffiti, faith of the poor.
Baskets of flowers and fruit, the head of black
Saint Jerome, tight hair radiating light
like spokes, the bright blues of another black
saint: St. Omer. His ears will ring now
with that rough singing, those bold strokes.

6. Love's reign

Some days it rained in spite of sun. Clouds
would gather in a moment to bring light showers or flood.
A storm broke late one night: she cried aloud.
He held her then as gently as he could
safe in the arms of love. When it was done,
that wind and driving rain, they were in love for good.
Railed now to that instinct, their lives would run
as one life on a double track. It would. It would.
You see that old couple in their kitchen?
They're still in love, watching the kettle boil
together, their passion steady as that hissing
steam, shining like a sheet of kitchen foil.
Tonight, watching the rain clouds gather above,
they'll celebrate the glory of the reign of love.

FIG VÈT

GEORGE GODDARD JR.

Fig vèt
èvèk fig vèt
èvèk fig vèt
èvèk an ti zandji dé lè
an zòdòmé obyen an kwab
lè nou alé la wivyè

É sé ti manmay-la mon dyé
sé dlo lowanjèt
dlo sikwé
é lannwit lè nou kouché
sé lavi sala nou ka sonjé
nou ka wévé…nou ka sonjé…lè nou lévé

Fig vèt
asou fig vèt
asou fig vèt
pitèt an ti zandji dé lè
an zòdòmé an kwab
lè nou alé la wivyè

(Green Fig

Green fig
and green fig
and green fig
sometimes with a bit of eel
or black river fish or crab
when we go by the river

and Lord, the children!
is orange leaf tea
or sweet water
and at night when we lie down
that life is in our dreams
we dream…we remember…when we wake

green fig
and more green fig
and more green fig
sometimes maybe a bit of eel
black river fish or crab
when we go by the river)

Translation by Kendel Hippolyte

IF I AM ANGRY

MELCHOIR HENRY

If I am angry
it is because our leaders
have betrayed us
it is because
they have played us
like kites into trees
they have made branches
poke holes
into our paper bodies;

If you see me
sulking on the lips of a river
hands beneath my cheek
it is because I have discovered
all are apparitions!

If I seek harbour
in society's dark hovels
it is because
I cannot face the sun
for lack of a cape
to spread over my naked skull

it is because
the tremulous din damages my eardrums
when I walk the streets
it is because
this island's reservoir
is a shallow basin;

If you see me
wavering when I walk
it is because some unseen cord
drags me towards
the tricksters' stage.

LIKE WIND

(August 19, 2001, Barbados)

KENDEL HIPPOLYTE

Hardest to understand
is that here too, there are seasons:
times of the harrowing of spirit, the dry days of no hope,
the lenten times when everything is fallow, waiting for the grace of rain.
To understand this is to know
that dying is a season also.
And knowing this you rest in the integrity of the unhandled world,
the manifest inexhaustibility of things, how trees keep dying into fruit,
how fruit keep dying into trees again without complaint,
how there is, always, earth.
But that understanding is a season also, is a grace.
It comes like wind, like wind you cannot hold it.
And if in its visitation, for the lived duration of a moment,
you see that everything — grass, lilies, the least hair on your head —
is moved by that same breath,
give thanks.

Dancing Pitons (2000)
Llewellyn Xavier

SPEAK YOUR MIND

RAS ISLEY

Look how other people ah shine
we murmuring, we grumbling, we staying behind.
If you can't talk, I'll talk for you!
Tell me nuh man, I'm in the struggle too.

    Speak your mind
    You won't speak your mind?
    Speak your mind

We unemployed, we want work
we want better pay
you afraid to lose your life sacrifice
say it once, say it twice
if you're not heard, say it thrice

    Speak you mind
    You won't speak you mind?
    Ah said, speak you mind

It's your democratic right, use it
tell government, tell opposition
tell man, woman, friend and enemy

tell management, tell mismanagement
tell them, say how you feel
you need a better deal
you don't want to steal

    Speak your mind
    You won't speak your mind?
    Speak your mind

You need a better life for your children
cost of living is getting higher
things ain't changing, ain't getting easier
the cry of the children getting louder

    Speak you mind
    You won't speak you mind?
    Speak you mind

Time to stand up and be brave
for your rights don't let them tell you how to behave
it's yourself and your future you got to save
shout! cry! let your voice be heard!

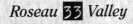

They say half a loaf is better than none
these days half a loaf is not even enough
The voice of the people is the voice of Jah
one day Jah will answer your prayer
but you must speak your mind

    You won't speak your mind?
    Speak your mind
    The Rasta will speak his mind.

 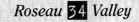

BREAKING COVENANT

BARBARA JACOBS SMALL

We have offered
holocausts of our hills—
still, we dare anticipate redemption
with their reluctant greening again.

Rivers are quiescent.
Their ancient acclamations constrict
in scorched catchments—
their praises drown in the babel
of our callous defiance.

The sun quenches
the last of night's anointing
on the moist lips of leaves—
unheard: the hosannas of itinerant ravines,
the hallelujahs of neglected streams.

And the land falls to desert,
and we repeat,
repeat,
convenient covenants.

PWÉZÈVÉ YO

MOSES 'MUSA' JN BAPTISTE

Ou kwè ou ja wè
an nich mal fini, kay zatolan?
Ou kwè ou konnèt an toutwèl
an kayali blan? Di mwen ki sa
ki an wanmyé, an jako, an kilibwi?
Wéponn mwen sa: koté mannikou, mangous, agouti?
Yonn ankò - sé maho nwè, powyé o bwa tan?

Ou wè ou pa konnèt tout sa
pas gwan gwan manman'w èk gwan gwan tonton'w
tjwé yo…èk fisi.
Pwézèvé yo…jenn jan
Pwézèvé yo…jenn jan
Lòt yo tjwé èk katapòl
pa menm an bwa ou sa jwenn pou fè sòl
pwézèvé yo…fama

Pas la pakay ni bwa
pa menm an jibyé pou fè tjè-mwen wi
jibyé, lawivyè, tout bèlté kay fini
pwézèvé yo…jenn jan.

Na kouté'w
ko lawivyè Twomasé, lawivyè Vyé Fò,
basen Tiwili, lawivyè Chwazèy?

Abwézan tout lawivyè sé sab èk wòch
tout lafowé sé WAP WAP èk koutla.
Koté kwibish basen, zòdòmé, zandji?
Kimanyè lawivyè go ka tèlman kako?
Yonn ankò - sé wavin, basen oben ma?

Ou wè ou pakay wè tou' sa
pas gwan manman'w èk gwan gwan tantant-ou
koupé yo èk koutla,
Pwézèvé yo…jenn jan.
Lòt yo tjwé èvèk gramoxone
pa menm an bouk pou fè an ti braf.

Pwézèvé yo…fama
pas la pakay ni dlo
pa menm an jibyé pou fè tjè-mwen wi
jibyé, lawivyè, tou' bèlté ka fini.

Ann' maché
ann' alé bò lanmè
gadé, nou sa konté gwenn sab-la
tout sab Bwa Chadon
sab anlè koko-a
kayè ka goumen èk dlo
dlo-a ka goumen èk kayè-a.

(Preserve them

You think you've ever seen a chicken hawk's nest, a ground dove's home? You think you know a dove, a white heron? Tell me what is a wood pigeon, a parrot, a hummingbird? Answer me this: where is the manicou, the mongoose, the agouti? Also, the black mahaut, the cedar, or the tree whose bark is used for tanning leather?

You see, you don't know all that. Because your great-great grandmother and great-great uncle killed them with guns. Preserve them, young people! Others they have killed with the catapult. You can't even find the wood to make house beams. You farmers, preserve them!

Because there'll be no trees, not even a bird to make my heart laugh. Birds, rivers, all the beauty will end. Preserve them, young people!

Listen to me. Where's the Troumassée River, the Vieux Fort River, the Tiwili Basin, the Choiseul River? Today, all rivers are sand and rocks. All forests—Wap! Wap!— the cutlass. Where are the crayfish, the black river fish, the eels? How come the big rivers are so brown? And the gullies, rock pools and ponds?

You see, you will not see all these. Because your grandmother and your great-great aunt destroyed them with cutlasses. Other things have been killed. Preserve them, young people. Other things have been killed with gramoxone. Not even a black shrimp to make a broth.

Farmers, preserve them! Because there won't be water. Not even a bird to make my heart laugh. Birds, rivers, all beauty will end. Walk with me. Let's go by the sea. Look, we can count the grains of sand, all the sand in Bwa Chadon, sand covering the coconuts. The rocks are fighting against the water, the water is fighting against the rocks).

Translation by Kendel Hippolyte

FLÈ WÒZ TJÈ MWEN

MARCIAN W.E. JN PIERRE

Apwé lapli-a tonbé
Sé ou ki lakansyèl mwen.
Si tout jan mwen voyé do asou mwen
Mwen ni èspwa ou kay la épi mwen.
Chak lè mwen gadé'w
Mwen ka wè sa mwen té ka mantjé-a.

Adanm pa té fèt pou viv pa kò'y
Alò, mwen pa té kay sa viv san ou.
Sé ou ki flè woz tjè mwen, doudou.

(Rose of my heart

After the rain has fallen
You are my rainbow
If all my friends turn their backs on me
I believe you will stay
Each time I see you
I see what it is I had been missing

Adam was not made to live alone
So I would not be able to live without you
Love, you are the rose of my heart)

Translation by Kendel Hippolyte

FOR FERGUS

JANE KING

When Fergus was dying, I had this fantasy
that when some people die, they ought to leave spaces
like holes in the air where they used to be.

Walking around quite normally, we'd stumble on these places
and choke and gasp in vacuum till the realization:
Oh! This is where he was. We need true memories, not just vague traces.

But well before he died, I'd feel a soul-deep irritation
when he would try to drift and they would shake him, trying to wring
a little more life from him. I wanted him to go with peaceful celebration.

I touched his body after they'd roped it in a sheet so porters could sling
it casually on to a barrow. He was not in it, though we felt him there
in the room. And walking down a common Castries street, later, I wanted to sing,

feeling his sudden joyous presence everywhere.
From far beyond his death, amazed, he sent a living blessing, tingling through the air.

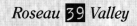

BIRTHDAY POEM

for Clifford Sealy

GEORGE LAMMING
Barbados

Today I would remember you whom birth brought no lucky dip
From which to pluck a permanent privilege,
And pain pushed prematurely into prose.
The photograph that recreates a child whose glance
Cast on the rescuing rock reads tyranny
His body bare to the bellowing wind
Has proved your former existence,
So when the season of awareness came
Passion made politics a serious game
And poverty your partner. How well I understood
The intolerant gesture, the juvenile lust to murder
An evil that had forged your life.

My birth records a similar story:
The freezing bastardy, the huddled tenantry,
Where children carry parents' pains like a uniform
Articulate only in their loyalty to life,
The individual desire or despair mocking most faithfully
Barometers that measure another's will,
And happiness as time indeed has shown
Absolved by the evil, intelligent question:
Was that piece of land a paying concern?

Those who start life without a beginning
Must always recall their crumbling foundations,
Rushing past affliction of the womb's unfortunate opening,
Reconsider now and again their earliest ambitions,
Or poised somewhere between loss and a possible arrival
Question their precarious present portion.
What new fevers arise to reverse the crawl
Our islands make towards their spiritual extinction?
Do you still patrol the city's unsavoury sites
Probing the prostitutes' hearts? Setting your intelligence
An exercise in pity as the warm nights
Drift their human flotsam before your questioning glance?

Nothing is changed in the news that reaches me here:
Papers continue to print the impossible, and rumours telegraph
Whatever falls within the senses' gauge.
Young poets are decorated with foreign approval
For precocious statements in a borrowed language,
Fashionable women whom comfort couldn't bless with sense
Still flock to applaud lectures by men
Who've a soft spot for the sound of their voices,
Corruption is keen; time throbs

With the ache of the proud and the sensitive like you
Who angrily wade through the vacuum
Forever afloat with oily seas,
While politicians posing incredible paunches
Parading their magical and primitive power
Fit the incompetent into jobs.

Life is similar in (what some call) the Mother Country
Where our people wear professions like a hat
That cannot prove what the head contains,
Success knows what grimace to assume,
Mediocrity is informed by a bright sense of bluff,
And Democracy a convenient attitude for many.
Students whom the huge city has shorn of glamour
Divorced from their status by a defect of colour
Find consolation in Saturday nights
With eloquent white whores that dance;
Or at nightfall over their new habit of tea
Argue with an elephant's lack of intelligence
Our culture must be spelt with a West Indian C.

We must suffer in patience whom life received
On islands cramped with disease no economy can cure,
Go with or without our lovers to the quiet shore
Where the reticent water weaves its pattern
And crabs crawl with a peculiar contemplation of the land,
Move through the multitude's monotonous cry
For freedom and politics at the price of blood,
Yet live every moment in the soul's devouring flame,
Until we fold with the folding earth,
Erect our final farewell in tree or cloud.
Hoping (if possible) for a people's new birth.

So you who care little for festival,
The seasonal sports, the carnival
Of barren souls in the February noon,
Preferring to inhabit your room, hoping to lean
On some durable solace in pages that justify
Your honest but innocent worship of the Russian regime
May not question why your exiled friend,
Seldom at ease in the habits of his time,
Never understanding why people pretend
To manufacture good wishes at certain times of the year,
Should yet try sincerely to offer you
A gift in words on your birthday.

WÉVOLOUSYON AN LAVI

DARNLEY LEBOURNE

Lézòm, dépi nou ti manmay
Nou tout ka annèk pòté chay
Lavi wèd, nou ka pwan fè
Tout bagay chè, nou ka soufè.

Chorus:
Tout bagay ka anèk wèd
Èk lavi difisil monchè
Débawé nou, débawé nou
É menm si nou pléwé
Bagay paka chanjé
Démawé nou, démawé nou.

Tjébé wèd, pa ladjé
Vini ansanm pou nou maché
Nou tout ni an twavay pou fè
Pou mété lavi-nou pli mèyè.

Chorus:

Atjwèlman sé wévolousyon
Sé sèl bagay pou solousyon
Wévolousyon – lavéwité

Wévolousyon – wéalité
Sé pou nou tout endiké nasyon-an
A la mannyè Wévolousyon.

(Revolution in life

Fellers, ever since we small
We just carrying a heavy load
Life hard, we ketching hell
Everything cost too much, we suffering

Chorus:
Everything just getting harder
And life difficult, my friend
Get out of our way, get out of our way
And even if we cry,
Things stay the same
Untie us, set us free

Hold on tight, don't let go
Let's come together so we can go forward
All of us have a work to do
So we can make our lives better

Chorus:

Right now it's revolution
It's the only solution
Revolution — that's the truth
Revolution — that's the reality
We all have to teach the nation
The way to revolution)

Translation by Kendel Hippolyte

FROM **CANTICLES**

JOHN ROBERT LEE

Canticle xv

Let us praise His Name with an opening lakonmèt,
and in the graceful procession of weedova;
let laughing, madras - crowned girls rejoice before Him in
the scottish
and flirtatious moolala, its violon hinting of heartache.
And while we forget time turning in quick-heeled polkas,
pause during the tentative norwegian —
for when the couples end the gwan won,
you alone must dance for Him your koutoumba.

Canticle xvi

I was glad when they call me to go up in the Séwénal.
The violon scraping my heart,
banjo and kwatro thrumming my grief like their plectrum,
and the guitar pulling my heel.
— I only seeing her tuning the mandolin on her bosom —
Then the chakchak shake me loose, insisting, insisting,
"wait for the bow, the bow and the courtesy,
wait for the sax, the drum and the kwadril to start." Selah.

Canticle xvii

And so, she has come: to the gold - flecked Wòb Dwiyèt,
its long train in folds over her left wrist,
the clean petticoat adorned with lace,
the satin foulard, the head-piece of rainbow madras —
from the nondescript costume of the far city,
from the profligate famine of Cardun's estates —
to the embracing plenitude of Kwadril chakchak and violon,
to that Bright Brooch on the glistening triangular foulard.

Canticle xx

And turning some Castries corner so familiar I don't even notice it,
on some day so unremarkable I don't recall it cool or hot —
distracted then by some matter of expenditure or composition or
was it passing lust,
I won't remember which. In any case, at leisure or in haste,
shall I turn the anonymous corner, on that day still to be lost,
to meet — the Lord Assassin — with my name in the
barrel of his fist?
Forget the avatar. Forget the extras diving under
sidewalk trays.
Today, your death will die. The Contract is paid. Selah.

Canticle xxi

What were they like, the last days of those buried cities —

Sodom, Pompeii, St. Pierre —
before the breasts salted in sulphur, scorched shards of precious
mosaic, orphaned sea-side avenues,
before the scattered ruin of temples, and villas gone to
charnel houses?

Thoroughly modern destinations — the women glamorous
and callous,
men corpulent in stampeding chariots, dance halls
promiscuous,
all the talk of scandals, crime, pestilential beggars,
and poets neglected, prophets tolerated.

On the familiar morning skyline,
the throat of the volcano dissolves in descending cloud.

Canticle xxii
After the promised irruption of heaven into earth
and subsequent looting of the enemy's barrows,
imagine — the astounded hurtling of hawk, the disconcerted
wonder of hen,
pup's amazement, astonished mule, kitten dumbfounded,
pipirit shocked! — And then, the heirs of God, cerement free,
parading the blue air. So great leviathan, cattle, creeping thing,
each to its kind,
rise without burden, with the lords of the air,

to come to their City, and their names calling out, from the
Lamb's Opening Book.

Canticle xxiii
Now He bears the image of His mother:
all-infolding eyes, smile settling at the lips' corners,
the rest of the face profoundly patient —
her Root, her Offspring, her Overshadowing Conception,
her Magnificent Annunciation, her Spirit-ravished Passion —

pondering liturgical mysteries, oppressed by the banal and the
tyrannical,
the children borne by this Incarnation
wait expectant as the willing will.

Canticle xxiv
Which is the 12th canticle —
The cascading words of my hand
pluck His praise from eight-string *bandlin* and local banjo,
place His favour on madras and foulard, the satin and the lace,
plant His steps in mazouk, lakonmèt and gwan won;
point His casual grace in yellow pumpkin star, pendular mango,
plait Him a crown of anthurium and fern —
He is the Crown, the Star of Grace, the Dancer of creation,
the Robing of righteousness, Tuning of the spheres, Hand of the
Incarnating Word. Selah.

LINES FOR A CONSERVATIVE

EGBERT LUCIEN

Something drumming now:
that throbbing fear of blank pages
white, fearsome spaces, not yet marked with my savage rage;

a throbbing fear that annihilates the coward
and his cold putrid complacence

until my fear swivels to a fierce anger
and I come to disturb your cool calm
armed with a yearning for truth;
the sweat of dew,
dawn's brightening cavalry
beating back dark phantoms of the night;
dawn's sky blood-stained with death and birth.

A bomb explodes somewhere
in the cool champagne of your suburb
shatters your clear, polished window of perception
to a splintered aftermath.

Horrified, drowning, you grope for straws;
greeted you at your door
and found you losing your balance
my memory framing a sagging drunk in that doorway
haggard, dishevelled, grinning stupidly
unmasking the true despair of your life.

and so the page must utter something
must proffer its morsel of truth
its images of dead and living things
its living metaphors of life and death
of joy and of sorrow
fears, hopes, illusions…

ETERNAL SLAVE

NKRUMAH AYODELE LUCIEN

Emancipation day done come, we gone and break de chains.
Me loose de shackle from I hand, but still cyan loose de brain.
Me freedom come de day we run from whip and cutting cane.
Me left de fields to village but me freedom gone again.

Me walk fast pace from place to place, still freedom I cyan find
Cause racist face I just replace with partial colour blind.
Immersed in inverse racism it wind up in de mind
As not a colour prejudice but "checking for I kind."

Black wife, black pride, black beautiful, repatriation too.
To where? To dat black motherland who haven't got a clue,
Since last the past shipwrecked her, where to find her lonesome crew
And remnants of a broken bridge for patriotic few?

Not here, I cyan find freedom yet, for race is not de place
And I cyan stand to drag me foot cause so much time I waste.
It eh take long till I get 'round to head back on me chase.
A higher heights done set me sight on freedom borne by grace.

It shackle I to book and law, to page, chapter and verse,
To "ignorance be blessed" and to "understanding cursed."
Well fastened to a faith not far from foolishness and worse
It won't welcome who won't conform to freedom well rehearsed.

Is freedom in religion where you have to fit de mold?
To "yours" alone devoted and to others just be cold?
To what you barely understand be loyal and be bold?
To there alone seek refuge from yourself and thus de world?

Is freedom when a man betray his hunger just to say
He eh go tief when at de time it was de only way
To bring de end to pain he feel and make dat urge decay?
Does freedom gnaw away at man until his fabrics fray?

I still in search of freedom and find shackle on I tongue.
Must always slave to language cause this master dere from long.
I slave meself to word and line to make me point more strong
So freedom must be slavery and is so me start me song:

If I man free from slavery I man slave to being free
Or to seeking I man freedom so a slave I man must be
If I don't slave to blindness I must slave to what I see
And till I left this life I must be slave to what I be.

Leo 'Spa' St. Helen (1927-1988)
Papa Jab (1958/59)

YÈ ÈK JÒDI

ARMELLE MATHURIN

Adan tan lontan
Lè nou pòkò té ni yon chay lajan
Mé nou té ni yon chay tan
Èk lamityé té gwan
Sent Lisyen té ka viv
Kon mòd la bib
Chaken pou lòt-la
Èk Dyé pou nou tout

Wèspé sé té yon fondasyon
Kòpowasyon sé té yon gwan endikasyon
Manmay té ni bon élivasyon
Èk moun té ka viv èvèk pokosyon
Sé té bonjou manman, bonjou papa,
Èskizé mwen, ès mwen sa alé la?
Padon, m'a tann sa'w di-a
Mèsi anchay, mwen apwésyé sa

Mé abwézan ni anchay konnésans
Lavi diféwan adan plizyé sans
Divès katjil, divès koumans
Chaken ni yon diféwan enflouans

Ni chay ki kwè éklawayson sé tout
Lòt kwè èk lajan lavi pa ni bout
É toujou yon kòpani kwè pozisyon sé mèt
Pou asiwé ou wété toujou a la tèt

Sé akonmsidi lakonpwann ja pèd valè
Lamityé èk pasyans ja téwé an tè
Padonnasyon èk pokosyon anchay kwè
Sé an tan pèdi èk yon gwan lèwè
Dèyè chak ti difikilté ni yon avoka
Tout kankan ka fini douvan majèstwa
Moun ka fè wòl, moun vini wézòl
Anchay ka fè akonmsidi yo fou oben fòl

Alò -
Anou pwan pokosyon èk sèvi bon wézon
An chay nou ka fè osijé endikasyon
Pas chak batisman yon jénéwasyon
Ka touvé plas anlè yon fondasyon
Ki té établi èk yon chay pokosyon
Pa ayèl avan pou yon bon wézon
Èk an pa jété pas I gadé vyé
Sa lézot joubaté telman wèd, pou yo té kite.

(Yesterday and today

In days gone by, when we didn't have much money, but we had a lot of time and our love was greater, Saint Lucians used to live as the Bible teaches. Each one for the other and God for all.

Respect was the foundation. Co-operation was the great education. Children had good upbringing and people lived carefully. It was: good morning mama, good morning papa. Excuse me, can I go there? I'm sorry, I didn't hear what you said. Thank you very much. I appreciate that a lot.

But nowadays, there's more knowledge. Life is different in many ways. Different ways of thinking, different ways of doing things, each one follows a different influence. A lot of people believe new thinking is all. Others think if you have money, life has no end. For still another set, social position is the most important thing to make sure you always come out on top.

It's as though understanding has no value. Love and patience are already buried in the earth. Forgiveness and carefulness, many think, are a waste of time, a huge mistake. At the end of every problem, there's a lawyer. Every quarrel ends up in front of a magistrate. People are not genuine. People have become hard. Many behave as though they are mad or crazy.

So – let us be careful and use our heads. Many of us are taking education seriously. Because every building that one generation finds is placed on a foundation which was laid with care by earlier people with good reason. One does not throw away, because it looks old, what others have struggled so hard to leave behind.)

Translation by Kendel Hippolyte

LAST SUPPER

YASMIN SOLITAHE ODLUM

My mother cooked
my father's death
one frustrated afternoon.
Cylindrical silver pot
brilloed to a scratchy shine
by our maid's industrious hands,
became a cauldron of bile
 bitterly brewing.

My meticulous mother
pouring bottles of oil
to vinegary water;
hot sauce boiling in,
scalding the pepper air,
curry powder, onions sliced,
garlic cloves,
and enough salt
to unskin a soucouyant
permanently.

For this last supper
she expected one guest.

She asked my father to drop in
to discuss matters,
dulcet voice innocent of potted plots.

Driving up the twin concrete strips
to meet her,
he parks, jauntily comes to the house
with greetings on his lips.

Sniffing the seasoned air
he pauses at the threshold of fragrant memories:
"Got something good cooking there.
Seems I'm just in time for dinner. Dear?"

My mother,
pot angled and angry
had waited
planned for so long
to bath down my hungry father.

She suddenly laughs
belly-deep, really strong
and lays her burden on the floor.

 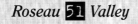

MY POEMS

LUCIUS PRESCOTT

I know my poems!

My poems don't taste like sugar apple and sapodilla.
They don't taste like star apple and ripe banana.
They don't taste like pine apple and sweet juicy guava.

I know my poems!

My poems taste like green tamarinds and granadilla.
They taste like gooseberries and green carambolla.
They taste like wild mushrooms and concentrated hemlock juice.

I know my poems!

My poems are not intimate hickies and friendly kisses.
My poems don't bite like honeybees and Jack Spaniards.
They bite like black sea-urchins and barnacles.
They bite like desert scorpions and tarantulas.
They bite like fer de lance and barracudas.
They bite like wild parrots
and hungry piranhas.

I know my poems!

My poems stink like rotten onions
and crushed bed bugs.
My poems aren't pretty dainty little things.
They are disgusting vicious ugly things.
They are carrion-eaters and blood-sucking vampires
set loose among the nations' high command and chiefs of staff.

I know my poems!
My poems aren't confetti.
They are wreaths!

MY.TIMES.IN.YOUR.HANDS.

LISA PROSPERE

a soughing creature in the womb I am
wailing silently, pushing anxiously

But then I look up and see
a beautiful beginning for the sun
and in the evening
a resplendent swan song.

Then I know my times are in Your Hands.

Waves crashing around in my head,
longing for a beginning
longing to be
broken on the shores of today.

And then I see rain coming
moon rising
wind blowing
life giving
of Your best
unfolded in Your plan
and then I know for sure
our. times. are. in. Your. Hands.

Father, if You timed my beginning
if You put me in this time and space
and 'til now have traced my life on the perfect pattern
of Your plan…
I'm content,
cuz my.times.are.in.Your.hands.

El Elyon
Who marries night with day
in the blazing portrait of the evening
and then rethinks the whole thing
in the pastel colors of the dawn…
I'm thankful for You, for my times
are beautifully, in Your Hands.

I'm a wave
I'll break on a shore
that's mine at a time
when the earth'll stand still for only me.
My times. You see. Are. In His Hands.

I'm a sky,
breaking slowly, slowly open
to display the awesome colors of my dawn.

 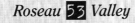

Day will break, I know
cuz my times are in His Hands.

I'm in Him and Him in me.
I'm timed, I'm poised
watching for the curtain call.
For when the lights go dim
the world will be waiting
for that time is. In His hands.

These same Hands
that speak forth planets
rotate night and light
orchestrate the crashing of the waves
and the coming of the tides
these same Hands
do now temper, nurture, feed and fan
my dreams, our love, my fire
for our performance on His stage
for.our.times.are.in.His.Hands.

INSIGHTS

ARTHUR A. RAYMOND

I. On the bright side

Sometimes, I marvel at my perfection.
I am, continually, surprised to find
I have two eyes and two ears, each
in the right place; and when I cut
myself, shaving, my blood clots.
Next day, new flesh will have grown.
I have two arms of equal length (approx.),
each terminating
in four fingers and an apposite thumb,
and their co-ordination is, absolutely, perfect.
Being male, my breasts remain, appropriately,
stunted; but I am, completely, served
by the machineries of joy.
Stomach and duodenum assimilate food,
reject, and process the unusable; and my liver
does whatever it is that livers do.
But, most of all, I wonder at the material,
enclosing me, like a bag, sensual with nerve-endings,
fitting, perfectly, and covering me, all over;
flexible, elastic, it would put any mac to shame:
my waterproof skin.

II. Return #2

Good man, well dig and deep;
Far down your quartered soul inside
the cave of recollection find.
Accumulated insults keep
their graces to your bandaged pride;
each surrogate of freedom hide
in solemn declarations kept unsigned.

Brave man far see and clear;
The convolutions of your sight
Do not let hide your future good.
Assimilate insights to hear
The promise of the morning light;
Loud let your heart be and bright
in simple resurrection of the blood.

PARASITE

HAZEL SIMMONS-MCDONALD

That tree has died.
Its topmost branches reach starkly heavenward
In seeming terror or mute supplication
To be rid of this vine that has clung
And drained it of existence.

Now its tendrils drape
The lifeless limbs to give itself
As gift in death a shroud
To the thing that gave it life.

How careless are the adornments of death.
Such irony
That in sustaining its own life
This vine has drained the very life it thrived upon.
It must be in all nature
To desire a death-in-life existence —
As we, shrouded in the foliage of passion,
Seek evanescent joy that
 only ends in death.

But there's one vine
Affixed upon a tree
That in death gave its life
To sundry branches.
It shall forever be our
Hope in life and
Life in death.

...BUT UNTIL THEN

KESTER SMALL

i. Too empty space
   for Columbia's crew

This scene is too serene for death.
I wish to change the weather,
take Titian's brush o'er length and breadth
of sky, and paint; forever

reflecting horror on the sea —
it should be bleeding, red,
shadowing tear-battened nimbuses,
a coagulum of lead.

The splendrous sun should be ashamed;
does he not hear the wails?
Does he not know that they have names?
The ones who exit on contrails?

Come now, oh darkness, blanket light
oh hurry to erase
this mocking brilliance from my sight,
this all too empty space.

ii. caterpillar time

Time's faithfulness often goes neglected,
a lowly caterpillar on its way
ignored, its true power unreflected
till late shall be revealed in light of day

so our days — though they may seem unnumbered
creep silently towards their destination
and, oh so slowly, they, unencumbered
will give birth, to the death, of all nations

so arise friends, lest when we have slumbered
awake to the last days of creation.

DON QUIXOTE

for George Odlum

GANDOLPH ST. CLAIR

I was pondering
Over his metaphor
The light familiarizing
The face of the actor
With eyes fanatic
Brow furrowed
Hands energetic
Body hallowed
Pied Piper on the stage
With Oxford gray hair
On the sports front page
Snatching the ball in mid air
The kick was powerful
The thrill of winning
Eloquence wonderful
Audience listening
Moving the passive
Present in the forum
To see you as massive
Without a quorum
In a cloak of ambition

You spurred the crusade
Knowing that the mission
Will in time be a façade
For at the ballots' count
You reflect on the loss
Don Quixote and his mount
Heading for Calvary's cross.

RUGGED VESSELS

PATRICIA TURNBULL

I've picked up many vessels
since that cracked one
was chucked away
the same for which I paid
too high a price.
There are the ornamental ones
gifts from the children
in fancy, gilded, oriental styles
with swirls and wings and petals
selected to appease.
There are the little ones
relieved from cluttered
gift-shop shelves
quaint souvenirs squeezed in
from places I can only
hope to see again.
And lately, I have learned
to make my own

pat-a-clay
pat-a-clay
maker's hands
make me a new woman
as fast as you can
moulded in my image
more than my children
want to be
the rugged beauty of each piece
holds my primordial sense
to make and multiply
to fill, to store, to know
to keep, to carry, to show
and yes, if it should come to this
to let weak vessels go.

ROSEAU VALLEY

for George Odlum

DEREK WALCOTT

A shovelful of blackbirds
shot over the road's shoulder
and memory twittered backwards
past the juddering steamroller

gravelling the asphalt road
this sunrise through Roseau
to the sugar mill that roared
to a stop and the widening echo

of canes, when they used to grow
cane in this sweet valley;
then from the canes in arrow,
blackbirds shot in volley

after volley of acolytes,
making every day Sunday
after the strike. No lights
on in the abandoned factory

now. Trolleys rust on ties.
The crop switched to bananas

instead and a boy's paradise
fell in sheaves of hosannas.

Between narrow gauge lines, grass
thickens. A crossing will wait
in vain for the old iron stanzas
to pass with their fragrant freight.

The factory's bleached galvanize
roof buckles. The sheets grapple
with crowbars of wind that prize
its last nails, but the chapel

at Jacmel, whose prayers gently chain
the joined wrists of workers (shoulders
still bent like the murmurous cane,
whatever the crop), stays as old as

the valley, and the litany
flows to the molasses accents
of local priests, not from Brittany
or Alsace-Lorraine. Incense

continues in the same vein
of charcoal smoke on a hill
connecting Roseau to heaven,
but breath went out of the mill.

How green and sweet I kept it
to my aging soul! It shines
when a muscular wind has swept it
with a shadowy scythe, but my lines

led to what? They provided
no comfort like the French priests'
or the Workers Hymn that divided
heaven from a wage increase,

this language that offered its
love few could read, those croppers
who shared communion's profits
or the Union's, for a few coppers.

What use was my praise of its level
green light to those valley-kind
folk? Over chimney and hovel
a cloud's fist closed and darkened

and gestured to the lightning
of crackling, amplified speeches
that broke into a roar of rain
from the irrigation ditches,

and the shirt-assembling flood
gathered in its full force
round the factory gate, then swirled,
bewildered at its next course.

Every scarecrow that had risen
from a ditch with crucified cry
would alarm the factory siren
or the eye of the belfry,

until, like dishevelled cane
after the crop was burnt,
their charred stalks threshed again
under Church and government,

but one Monday road-wide
they marched, sheaves in the fist,
as police bikes purred beside
them towards Government Office,

and the brown river flowed up uphill,
its noise coiled round the Morne,
and it left the old sugar mill
to look after its cane alone.

My hand shared the same unrest as
the workers, but what were its powers
to those ragged harvesters
turning my Book of Hours?

Demons snarl in a flag and
smoke coils from a thurifer,
the breath of the opium dragon
makes a Lenin of Lucifer.

Countries of cereal grain
are swept under the shadow
of a scything flag, so the cane
went with the blackbird's arrow,

and, gone with its harvest, what?
My vision that made it once
"orient and immortal wheat"
or the height of indifference?

But was mine a different realm
really? Mitres or pawns can shift
the shadows of a changing regime
over square fields, but my gift

that cannot pay back this island
enough, that gave no communion
of tongues, whose left hand
never lifted the sheaves in union,

still sweats with the trickling resin
in a hill's hot armpit, as
my choice of a road is rising
from the sea's amphitheatres

to inhale a bracing horizon
above belfry or chimney where
the steamroller's heartbeat dies on
blue, indivisible air.

TETE CHEMIN

for Lester "Starch" Andrew

TRAVIS WEEKES

A bend in the road
simply a bend in that potholed road
stretched shortly into a hill
a lull-a rumshop-a rest
Victor – grown on bananas
growing bananas – golden bananas
climbing hills – forking dirt
rooting stems
pleasing the British palate

Bananas plants
worded over hillsides
spelled over plains
leafy green and dancing in sunlight
punctuating uncaringly – children's classes

"Gadé mwen Misyé teacha
hich-mwen passa vini l'ékòl jòdi-a
pas i ni pou aidé mwen épi sé fig-la"

Tete Chemin
simply a bend in the road
Millet snaked to a full-stop
cornered into a rum-shop
There, children trail their elders

into the sweat and gamble of fig
ploughing, planting – rooting their family bet;
at night the trail and gamble unfinishes into
"Gwen dé
dé shot"

Sad temptations for the intruder of a poet
idly turning a yellow fig into a
quarter moon and romanticizing his rising lust
for the rounded females of the fig

For Victor
yellow bananas are the moon too
only last quarter
he has already missed school on banana days
having realized that banana boxes
are the "New Capital Arithmetic"

Tete Chemin
simply a bend in the road
but still
lettered with children
whose dreams drip with tears
trying always to fit figs together
to make a full moon.

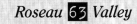

St. Lucia Arts Guild production (1968) - The Sea at Dauphin by Derek Walcott.
From l to r, George Odlum, Howick Elcock and Eric Brandford.

EPILOGUE

ODE TO AN ARTIST

CHARLES CADET

Pa pléwé ban mwen
Pa pòté dèy mwen
Lam mwen libéwé
Lèspwi déchènné

Menm kon an ti mèl
Zèl sispann an syèl
Lam mwen libéwé
Lèspwi déchènné

Chanté kont-la ban mwen
Pòté wonm blan-a
Pasé kafé-a
Kité listwa di
Tim-tim - Bwa chèz!
Dlo sispann – koko
Tim-tim – Bwa chèz!
Dlo doubout – sé kann
Tim-tim – Bwa chèz!
Ki sa Bondyé mété asou latè-a?

Ki sa Bondyé mété asou latè-a?
Tout chòz
Kité listwa di
Lavi pa ka fini
Lavi ka kontiné
Lamò pa ka genyen
Pa limen chandèl
Lavi imòtèl
Lam mwen libéwé
Lèspwi déchenné
Pa pléwé ban mwen
Pa pòté dèy mwen

(Òmaj pou an atis

Don't cry for me
Don't mourn for me
My soul is free
My spirit, unchained

Like a little blackbird
Soaring in the heavens
My soul is free
My spirit, unchained

Sing the kont for me
Bring the white rum
Pass round the coffee
Let the storytelling start:
Tim-tim – bwa chèz
Hanging water? – Coconut!
Tim-tim – bwa chèz
Standing water? – That's cane!
Tim-tim – bwa chèz
What has God put on earth?
What has God taken from the earth?
Everything.

Let the storytelling start.

Life has no end
Life goes on
Death will not win
Don't light any candles for me
Life is immortal

My soul is free
My spirit is unchained
Don't cry for me
Don't mourn for me)

Translation by Kendel Hippolyte

Contributors

Harold Simmons (1914-1966), regarded by many as the father of the arts and culture of modern St. Lucia. He led the arts and crafts movements of the forties, was a mentor to Derek Walcott, Dunstan St. Omer, Leo 'Spar' St. Helene and their generation. He is credited with 'discovering' Sessenne Descartes. He was a painter, journalist, archaeologist, linguist, anthropologist, in a short life that held much in its hands. He is the guiding spirit of the Folk Research Centre, St. Lucia and its 30 year work.

Dunstan St. Omer, veteran St. Lucian painter, especially famous for his Madonnas and church murals. Popularly known as 'Apilo,' he holds a central place in Walcott's long poem 'Another life.'(1972)

Leo 'Spa' St. Helene (1927-1988), St. Lucian photographer and sportsman, whose photographs of an earlier St. Lucia provide a valuable archive of past social and cultural life.

Virginia Henry, with a distinctive painting style, originally from the United Kingdom, has made her home in St. Lucia for many years.

Llewellyn Xavier, originally from Choiseul, is St. Lucia's internationally famous modern painter.

Corine George, one of St. Lucia's new crop of talented artists. Her *'Kabawé'* provides the cover illustration.

Msgr. Dr. Patrick Anthony, familiarly known as 'Paba' is a St. Lucian priest and folklorist, the founder of the Folk Research Centre. Both his Masters and Doctoral dissertations examined the theological aspects of the work of Derek Walcott. He is Chairman of the Jubilee Trust Fund.

Dame Marie Sessenne Descartes, popularly known as the 'Queen of Folk' in St. Lucia, is the island's best known folk singer.

Charles Cadet, singer and song-writer, was a collaborator for many years with the late Roderick Walcott on plays like Banjo man and other unique St. Lucian musical theatre. Many of his songs are St. Lucian classics.

George 'Fish' Alphonse, actor, director and St. Lucia's leading performance poet. He is responsible for organizing the annual La Rose and La Magrit flower festivals.

Adrian Augier, economist, painter, carnival designer, actor, director. He has published a number of collections of poetry. *Bridgemaker* (2001) is his latest publication.

Edward Baugh, Jamaican poet, university lecturer, literary critic. He has written a number of articles and books on the work of Derek Walcott.

John Blanchard, now resident in the USA, was among the active poets in St. Lucia in the seventies and eighties.

Kamau Brathwaite, Major Caribbean and Barbadian poet, whose innovative style and themes make him the most distinctive of his generation. He has published several volumes of poetry, many articles on Caribbean literature, and books and monographs on Caribbean history. He was Extra Mural Tutor of the University of the West Indies in St. Lucia in 1963.

Martin Carter (Guyana, 1927-1998), poet and politician whose poems led the call for independence from colonial masters.

Tassia Channel Clement, one of the new wave of St. Lucian writers. She is a member of the St. Lucia Writers' Forum.

Melania Daniel, economist by profession, has also written plays which have been performed. Her poetry collection *Mindfield* was published in 1994.

Anderson Desir, a prolific poet from the sixties, whose work can be found mainly in newspapers, small magazines and some international anthologies.

Irvin Desir, called by some of his contemporaries "a poet's poet." His work can be found in *Confluence* (1988), an anthology of St. Lucian poetry edited by Kendel Hippolyte.

Sheila Desmond, Burmese national, resident in Manhattan.

Mac Donald Dixon, a bridge between the Walcott generation and the newer poets of the seventies. He has written plays as well as poetry. His *Collected Poems* (1961-2001) was published in 2002. He is the author of a novel, 'Season of mist' (2001). He has won prizes for his photography.

J. Edsel Edmunds, a scientist by training, diplomat by profession, and former St. Lucian Ambassador to the United Nations, is a painter and poet whose collection *Many Horizons* was published in 2000.

Hunter J. Francois, lawyer and politician, former Minister of Education in St. Lucia, published his only collection of poetry, *First and Last poems* in 1949. Introduction and cover design were by Derek Walcott.

Stanley French, St. Lucian playwright whose plays have been performed regionally and internationally. He is an engineer by profession. He has been awarded the St. Lucia Medal of Merit (Gold) for his contribution to the arts.

Michael Gilkes (Guyana), was resident for many years in St. Lucia. Professor of Literature, he has published a number of books on Caribbean literature. His first collection of poetry *Joanstown* was published in 2002.

George Goddard Jr., is a trade unionist by profession. His poem Fig vèt was one of the first popular poems in St. Lucian Kwéyòl. He is working on a first collection.

Melchoir Henry, one of the 'angry young men' of the eighties, published his *Dead country* in 1981.

Ronald 'Boo' Hinkson, one of St. Lucia's best known guitarists, songwriters and leader of the popular Tru Tones in the sixties and seventies. He has recorded several albums. His styles range across all forms of music, from folk to calypso to reggae. He is also well known on the international jazz circuits. His most recent CD is entitled *Beyond* (2003).

Kendel Hippolyte, poet, playwright, actor, director, literature teacher, has been an inspiration to his contemporaries and students. His latest collection is *Birthright* (Peepal Tree, 1997) A new collection, *Night Vision* is forthcoming from Northwestern University Press, Illinois.

Ras Isley, a rapso poet, is also an actor. Several of his poems have been recorded on CD.

barbara jacobs-small, well known in St. Lucia as a radio personality, manages her own advertising agency, Right Angle Imaging.

Moses 'Musa' JnBaptiste, school principal in Vieux Fort in southern St. Lucia, is a member of the performance poetry group Tambou Mélé.

Marcian W.E. JnPierre, has been a leading translator of several St. Lucian Kwéyòl publications. He is a member of the St. Lucia Writers' Forum.

Jane King, literature teacher, has published several articles on Caribbean literature. Her latest publication is *Fellow Traveller* (1994).

George Lamming, Barbadian novelist, among whose novels is the classic *In the castle of my skin* (1953).

Darnley Lebourne, St. Lucian environmentalist, among the first poets of the seventies and eighties to popularize Kwéyòl performance poetry.

John Robert Lee, Christian poet, newspaper columnist and preacher has also worked in library management and media. His latest collection is *Artefacts* (2000).

Egbert Lucien, one of the strong voices of the eighties, his work can be found in *Confluence* (1988).

Nkrumah Ayodele Lucien, (son of Egbert Lucien) is one of the new voices in St. Lucian writing. He is a member of the St. Lucia Writers' Forum.

Armelle Mathurin, cultural activist from Mon Repos on the south-east coast of St. Lucia, has been a school principal and promoter of the use of St. Lucian Kwéyòl.

Yasmin Solitahe Odlum, a former literature teacher, is one of St. Lucia's diplomats in Washington. She is a daughter of George Odlum.

Lucius Prescott, a frequent winner of the annual M&C Fine Arts Awards in St. Lucia, has written several poetry manuscripts.

Lisa Prospere, literature teacher and television personality in St. Lucia, is among the new writers of St. Lucia, and a member of the Writers' Forum.

Arthur A. Raymond, first published in the UK in an anthology entitled Breaklight (1971), is one of St. Lucia's unknown writing talents. He is a computer specialist in St. Lucia.

Hazel Simmons-McDonald, St. Lucian lecturer at the Cave Hill Campus, UWI. Her forthcoming collection is entitled *Silk cotton and other trees* (Ian Randle 2003).

Kester Small, one of the new writers, is a member of the Writers' Forum.

Gandolph St. Clair, actor, playwright, singer and song writer, has published several volumes of poetry and prose. His latest work is *Firefall* (2002).

Patricia Turnbull, St. Lucian Professor of Literature living in Tortola, published her first collection *Rugged vessels* in 1992.

Derek Walcott, St. Lucian poet, playwright, essayist, director, painter, won the Nobel Prize for Literature in 1992. His latest book of poetry is *Tiepolo's Hound* (2000). His most recent collection of plays is *The Haitian Trilogy* (2002).

Travis Weekes, a literature teacher, also directs theatre. His collection of poetry is entitled *Let there be jazz* (1997)

© Acknowledgements

The editor and publisher are grateful to the following copyright holders for permission to reproduce their poems and/or song lyrics:

Dame Marie Sessenne Descartes for *Nou tout sé menm;* Charles Cadet for *Poinsettia Blossoms* and *Ode to an artist*; Ronald 'Boo' Hinkson for *Burning eyes and hungry bellies*; George 'Fish' Alphonse for *Forget dem old ting*; Patrick A.B. Anthony for *Twilight;* Adrian Augier for *Comerette*; Edward Baugh for *Black sand*; John Blanchard for *Fading lifestyle*; Kamau Brathwaite for *The visibility trigger*; Phyllis Carter for *Proem* by Martin Carter; Tassia Channel Clement for *Under the sun*; Melania Daniel for *Mystery lover*; Anderson Desir for *I have flung fire*; Irvin Desir for *from Islander*; Sheila Desmond for *Overheard*; Mac Donald Dixon for *Fallen angel*; J.Edsel Edmunds for *Them and I*;Hunter Francois for *Johnny and I*; Stanley French for *Fern Gully*; Michael Gilkes for *Sonnets*; George Goddard jr. for *Fig vèt*; Melchoir Henry for *If I am angry*; Kendel Hippolyte for *Like wind*; Ras Isley for *Speak your mind;* Barbara Jacobs Small for *Breaking covenant*; Moses 'Musa' JnBaptiste for *Pwézèvé yo*; Marcian W.E. JnPierre for *Flè wòz tjè mwen*; Jane King for *For Fergus*; George Lamming for *Birthday poem*; Darnley Lebourne for *Wévolousyon an lavi*; John Robert Lee for *from Canticles*; Egbert Lucien for *Lines for a conservative*; Nkrumah Ayodele Lucien for *Eternal slave*; Armelle Mathurin for *Yè èk jòdi*; Yasmin Solitahe Odlum for *Last supper;* Lucius Prescott for *My poems*; Lisa Prospere for *my.times.in.your.hands.*; Arthur A. Raymond for *Insights*; Hazel Simmons-McDonald for *Parasite;* Kester Small for *...but until then*; Gandolph St. Clair for *Don Quixote*; Patricia Turnbull for *Rugged vessels*; Derek Walcott for *Roseau Valley*; Travis Weekes for *Tete Chemin*.

National Community Foundation

Remarks

National Community Foundation

The National Community Foundation is a non-profit, non-governmental organization that seeks to raise funds through contributions from donors be it private citizens, local corporations, other foundations and government agencies.

The NCF functions primarily as a grant making institution, supporting a wide range of charitable and social development activities that creatively address emerging and changing community needs in such fields as education, arts and culture, health, social services, community development, environment and civic affairs.

The financial instability in the region has resulted in the creation of a 'new poor' in the region. These are the group that finds itself most affected by the high incidence of unemployment and company 'right-sizing'. This new group added to the group who are already living below the poverty line, dramatically increases the percentage of St. Lucians who are finding it impossible to make ends meet on a daily basis.

Ironically, the truly talented within the artistic community too often fall within the realm of the "poor." NCF, like the Jubilee Trust Fund is concerned that the artists in modern communities operate within a recognized and viable economic sector. Their craft carries worth and their contributions are justly compensated. The NCF, Like the Jubilee Trust Fund, appreciates and acknowledges the role of the artist in the archiving of culture.

This project, with its various objectives, is development driven. It is significant in the context of the historical times of the country. Moreso, it will have a timeless shelf life. If incorporated into the literature curriculum, it will significantly assist in the nurturing of a St. Lucian cultural identity at the right age; it will also legitimize the St. Lucian character, through education. It has an income-generating component that speaks to sustainability, and it promises new opportunity for the new voices published alongside recognized names. NCF says "well done" to the Jubilee Trust Fund.

Barbara Jacobs Small
Public Relations Subcommittee
National Community Foundation

George Odlum
(October 2002)

Photo by Solitahe Odlum

George Odlum
(October 2002)

Photo by Solitaire Odlum